Collins English Readers

Amazing Explorers

Level 3
CEF

D1240410

Text by
Anne Collins

Series edited by
Fiona MacKenzie

Collins

HarperCollins Publishers
77–85 Fulham Palace Road
Hammersmith London W6 8JB

10 9 8 7 6 5 4 3 2 1

Original text
© The Amazing People Club Ltd

Adapted text
© HarperCollins Publishers Ltd 2014

ISBN: 978-0-00-754497-4

Collins® is a registered trademark of
HarperCollins Publishers Limited

www.collinselt.com

A catalogue record for this book is available
from the British Library

Printed in the UK by Martins the Printers

HarperCollins does not warrant that
www.collinselt.com or any other website

mentioned in this title will be provided
uninterrupted, that any website will be
error free, that defects will be corrected, or
that the website or the server that makes it
available are free of viruses or bugs. For full
terms and conditions please refer to the site
terms provided on the website.

These readers are based on original texts
(BioViews®) published by The Amazing
People Club group.® BioViews® and The
Amazing People Club® are registered
trademarks and represent the views of the
author.

BioViews® are scripted virtual interview
based on research about a person's life and
times. As in any story, the words are only
an interpretation of what the individuals
mentioned in the BioViews® could have
said. Although the interpretations are
based on available research, they do not
purport to represent the actual views of
the people mentioned. The interpretations
are made in good faith, recognizing that
other interpretations could also be made.
The author and publisher disclaim any
responsibility from any action that readers
take regarding the BioViews® for educational
or other purposes. Any use of the BioViews®
materials is the sole responsibility of the
reader and should be supported by their own
independent research.

Cover image © haveseen/Shutterstock

MIX
Paper from
responsible sources
FSC **FSC® C007454**
www.fsc.org

Find out more about HarperCollins and the environment at
www.harpercollins.co.uk/green

◆ CONTENTS ◆

Collins Amazing People Readers are collections of short stories. Each book presents the life story of five or six people whose lives and achievements have made a difference to our world today. The stories are carefully graded to ensure that you, the reader, will both enjoy and benefit from your reading experience.

You can choose to enjoy the book from start to finish or to dip in to your favourite story straight away. Each story is entirely independent.

After every story a short timeline brings together the most important events in each person's life into one short report. The timeline is a useful tool for revision purposes.

Words which are above the required reading level are underlined the first time they appear in each story. All underlined words are defined in the glossary at the back of the book. Levels 1 and 2 take their definitions from the *Collins COBUILD Essential English Dictionary* and levels 3 and 4 from the *Collins COBUILD Advanced English Dictionary*.

To support both teachers and learners, additional materials are available online at www.collinselt.com/readers.

The Amazing People Club®

Collins Amazing People Readers are adaptations of original texts published by The Amazing People Club. The Amazing People Club is an educational publishing house. It was founded in 2006 by educational psychologist and management leader Dr Charles Margerison and publishes books, eBooks, audio books, iBooks and video content which bring readers 'face to face' with many of the world's most inspiring and influential characters from the fields of art, science, music, politics, medicine and business.

◆ The Grading Scheme ◆

The Collins COBUILD Grading Scheme has been created using the most up-to-date language usage information available today. Each level is guided by a brand new comprehensive grammar and vocabulary framework, ensuring that the series will perfectly match readers' abilities.

		CEF band	Pages	Word count	Headwords
Level 1	elementary	A2	64	5,000–8,000	approx. 700
Level 2	pre-intermediate	A2–B1	80	8,000–11,000	approx. 900
Level 3	intermediate	B1	96	11,000–15,000	approx. 1,100
Level 4	upper intermediate	B2	112	15,000–18,000	approx. 1,700

For more information on the Collins COBUILD Grading Scheme, including a full list of the grammar structures found at each level, go to www.collinselt.com/readers/gradingscheme.

Also available online: Make sure that you are reading at the right level by checking your level on our website (www.collinselt.com/readers/levelcheck).

Marco Polo

◆ ◆

*c.*1254–1324

the man who taught the world about China

**I was the greatest European traveller of my time.
I journeyed to China along the <u>Silk Road</u>, and lived
there for many years in the service of Kublai Khan.
I wrote a book about my travels which <u>inspired</u>
Christopher Columbus.**

◆ ◆ ◆

I was born in the city of Venice, Italy, into a rich <u>merchant</u> family. My father and uncle were Niccolò and Maffeo Polo, <u>traders</u> who bought and sold <u>goods</u> from different places around the world. At the time of my birth, Niccolo and Maffeo were away on a long journey, and didn't return to Venice until 1269. In those days, when traders made journeys, they often didn't come home for a long time. Sometimes they died on the way and didn't come home at all. My mother died when I was young, and I was looked after by other people in my family. But I didn't meet my father and my uncle until I was 15 years old.

My father and uncle told me wonderful stories about the amazing places they'd visited, and the people they'd met on their travels. In 1253, they'd sailed to Constantinople, an important city for traders from around the world. They'd stayed there for six years, then they'd travelled east through many countries, eventually reaching the city of Bukhara, in the country now known as Uzbekistan. At that time, Bukhara was an important city on the famous Silk Road. Niccolò and Maffeo stayed there for three years, <u>trading</u> their goods. Then they met an important <u>official</u> who was travelling to China to meet the great and powerful Mongol ruler of China, Kublai Khan. He invited my father and uncle to go with him to China, so they set off together along the Silk Road.

The Silk Road wasn't just one road, but a route made up of a number of roads between China and Europe. It was about 6,500 kilometres long, and hundreds of years old. It was very important for <u>trade</u>, because merchants used it to bring <u>silk</u>, <u>spices</u>, jewels and other goods from the countries of the East to Europe. The journey was long and difficult, and sometimes very dangerous. Travellers could be attacked by thieves or wild animals, or they could die from diseases. In order to protect themselves, merchants often travelled together in large groups called caravans. They rode on <u>camels</u> or horses, stopping from time to time along the way at places called 'caravanserais'. Here they could find food and rest, and meet other travellers.

◆ ◆ ◆

In 1264, after a long journey, my father and uncle arrived at Kublai Khan's palace in the city of Khanbaliq (now known as Beijing). Kublai Khan was the grandson of the great Genghis Khan, and the most powerful man in the Mongol <u>Empire</u>. He was very pleased to meet Niccolò and Maffeo, and asked them many questions about European countries. He wanted to know about these countries' systems of politics and law, and their other traditions too. My father and uncle developed a good relationship with Kublai Khan, and traded successfully in China for two years. When they left, the Khan made them promise to return, and gave them a special gold passport. This would show people that they were under the Khan's protection, so that nobody would hurt them. In addition, it meant that they would be offered food and a place to stay on their journey.

Kublai Khan was also very interested in the Pope, the head of the <u>Catholic Church</u>, who lived in Rome. He asked Niccolò and Maffeo if they would take a letter to the Pope, and bring back a hundred <u>priests</u> to China who could teach mathematics and science. In addition, he asked them to bring oil from the famous Church of the <u>Holy</u> Sepulchre in Jerusalem. Niccolò and Maffeo promised to bring both the priests and the oil. As soon as they returned to Venice in 1269, they started to plan their return journey to China. I was very excited because they'd told me that they'd take me with them. We left Venice in 1271, and sailed south to Acre, a town on the Mediterranean Sea about 130 kilometres from Jerusalem. From there we travelled to the Church in Jerusalem, and got the oil.

Although we had the oil, getting the priests was more of a problem. The old Pope had died and a new one, Pope Gregory the Tenth, was now head of the Catholic Church.

Merchants travelled in large groups called caravans

He sent us some letters to take to Kublai Khan, but he only sent two priests to go with us, not a hundred! Unfortunately, these priests found the journey very difficult, and quickly decided to go back home. We were worried that Kublai Khan might not be pleased with us if we arrived without the priests, but we decided to continue our journey. We travelled through the countries now known as Turkey, Georgia, Iran and Iraq, to Hormuz, where we were hoping to find a ship to take us to China. However, there was no suitable ship, so we continued our journey by land, along the Silk Road.

♦ ◆ ♦

Along the way, I was learning valuable lessons from my father and uncle about the skill of trading. They showed me how to buy goods in some markets at a low price, then sell them in other markets at a higher price. It was especially difficult to trade in languages that I didn't understand! We journeyed on to Badakhshan (in the country now known as

Afghanistan) but here I became very ill. Niccolò and Maffeo waited for many months for me to get better, but still I wasn't well enough to travel. At last, they took me away from the desert and high up into the cold air of the Pamir mountains, where finally I began to feel well again. We continued travelling east, until we came to the Gobi Desert, a huge area of sand which was very difficult to cross safely.

People said that the Gobi Desert was so wide that it would take a whole year to get from one side to the other. However, we crossed it at the narrowest point, which took about a month. The desert consisted entirely of mountains and valleys and sand. It was an empty place where there was nothing at all to eat. Finally, we got to the other side and arrived safely in the city of Suchow, the first large city after the desert, where we stayed for a year. By this time, we'd been travelling for three years, but we still needed to travel further east to meet Kublai Khan. At last, we reached his <u>magnificent</u> summer palace at Xanadu, with its beautiful parks and animals. The Khan was delighted to see us, and welcomed us in a friendly way.

The Khan was very pleased with the oil and the letters from the Pope. Fortunately, he wasn't angry that we hadn't been able to bring the hundred priests. He asked who I was, and from the time that I was introduced to him, he took a great interest in me. I was amazed by the wonderful things I saw at the Khan's palace, and the great respect his people had for him. He got his wealth from the taxes which his people paid, and he used the money to benefit them as well as himself. Every December, the Khan moved his <u>court</u> to the winter palace in the city of Khanbaliq. Khanbaliq was surrounded by four walls and each wall was almost ten kilometres long. There were twelve entrances guarded by soldiers and in the centre of the city was the winter palace with hundreds of rooms for the Khan and his wives.

◆ ◆ ◆

I learned to read and write the Khan's language and several other languages too, and I became familiar with Chinese traditions. I quickly became one of the Khan's favourites, the people he liked and trusted most. I was <u>impressed</u> not only by the wealth and beauty of his palaces, but also by the new things I saw there, such as the use of paper money. The money was printed in a special place called the Khan's Mint, and was used for trading in every corner of his empire. This was the first time I'd seen paper money, and I thought it was an excellent idea.

Kublai Khan's empire produced many things, such as iron and salt, and these goods were quickly transported by large boats. There was an excellent system of communication, so that messages could be taken from place to place very quickly. There were message stations every 40 kilometres along the road, where riders on horses waited. When a rider arrived at a station with a message, another rider then took it on to the next station. In this way, a message could be carried hundreds of kilometres in a day. We decided that there were 10,000 message stations in China.

Kublai Khan needed someone to travel around his huge empire, and to represent him <u>officially</u> as his <u>ambassador</u>. He liked and trusted me very much, so in 1275, he asked me to visit some places in his empire, and report to him what was happening. I wanted to do a good job, so I wrote down careful descriptions of everything I saw, and when I returned from my travels, the Khan was very pleased with me. During the next 17 years, I journeyed to many places for the Khan and became a very important man. I had a gold passport and fine clothes, and travelled with many servants. I visited the countries now known as Burma, India, Vietnam and Sri Lanka. In addition, from 1282 to 1287, I was the governor of the city of Yangzhou, which was a great honour.

But after 17 years, although we'd greatly enjoyed our time in China, my father and uncle were keen to go home to Venice. We'd enjoyed a very good relationship with the Khan for many years, but now he was an old man, and Niccolò and Maffeo were worried about would happen to us after he died. They knew that some people at his court were jealous of us, and they were afraid that these people might become our enemies. However, every time we asked the Khan if we could leave and go back to Venice, he refused to let us go.

◆ ◆ ◆

At last our chance came in 1292, when the Khan asked us to accompany a beautiful princess to Kerman in Persia (the country now known as Iran). The ruler of the Mongol Empire in Persia was looking for a wife, and the Khan had agreed to send him a princess from his court. The Khan ordered us to accompany the princess to Kerman, and take her to her future husband. He gave us permission to continue on to Venice, but after that he made us promise to return to China. We agreed, and in 1292, we set sail from the city of Zaitun with a fleet of 14 large ships. But the journey took

The Route of Marco Polo

two years, and was very difficult and dangerous. Our ships often <u>ran into</u> bad weather, and many people died because of storms, accidents or diseases.

At last we reached Kerman, where we said goodbye to the princess. Then we set off for Venice, but on the way we received the sad news that Kublai Khan had died. We realized that this was the end of our travels to China because we could never live there safely without the protection of the great Khan. So we continued our journey home, and arrived back in Venice in 1295, after 24 years. I'd been a young boy of 17 when I first left Venice, and now I was a man of 41. It had been so many years since we left, that our families believed that we were dead, and they didn't recognize us. But we'd brought back jewels and gold from our travels, and we were now very rich merchants.

We found that the Italian cities of Venice and Genoa were at war. They were fighting about trade routes in the Mediterranean Sea. I fought for Venice, and in 1298 I was taken prisoner by the Genoans and put in prison. There I met a man called Rustichello da Pisa. We became good friends, and I told him about my <u>adventures</u>. Rustichello wrote down my story in a book, which was later called, in English, *The Travels of Marco Polo*, and was read by many people, including Christopher Columbus. After I was released from prison in August, 1299, I realized that my travels were over and it was time to begin a new life at home. So I started a trading company with my father, and married Donata Badoer, the daughter of a rich merchant. Later, Donata and I had three daughters. I lived peacefully in Venice until my death from an illness in 1324 at the age of 70.

The Life of Marco Polo

c.1254   Marco Polo was born in Venice, Italy while his father, Niccolò, and uncle, Maffeo, were away on a trading journey to China. After Marco's mother died, he was looked after by other members of his family.

1264   Niccolò and Maffeo Polo arrived at Kublai Khan's palace in the city of Khanbaliq (now Beijing).

1269   Niccolò and Maffeo returned home to Venice, and met 15-year-old Marco for the first time.

1271–1275   Marco, Niccolò and Maffeo made the long and dangerous journey along the Silk Road to China. They arrived at Kublai Khan's Palace in Xanadu, and started working for him. Marco became the Khan's ambassador and started making official visits to places in his empire.

1282–1287   Marco served as Governor of the City of Yangzhou.

1292   Marco, Niccolò and Maffeo sailed from Zaitun in China, in order to take a princess from the Khan's court to Persia to get married.

1295   After the death of the Khan, the Polos arrived back in Venice after 24 years.

1298   Marco fought for Venice against the Genoans, but was taken prisoner. While he was in prison, he met Rustichello da Pisa, who wrote down the stories of his adventures, later published in a book called *The Travels of Marco Polo.*

1299–1300   Marco was freed from prison. He married Donata Badoer. Later they had three children and he became a wealthy merchant.

1324   Marco died in Venice from an illness at the age of 70.

Ibn Battuta

◆ ◆ ◆

1304–*c*.1369

the man who travelled to 44 countries

**I lived a long time ago but my name is very famous.
I travelled to most countries in the Muslim world. I had
many <u>adventures</u> and survived great dangers. I recorded
everything I saw in a book about my travels.**

◆ ◆ ◆

I was born in Tangier, on the northern coast of Morocco, on 24th February 1304. My family came from the Berber <u>tribe</u> and were <u>scholars</u> in Islamic law, so I was educated in Islamic law. In June 1325, at the age of 21, I set off on the *hajj*, or <u>pilgrimage</u> to the <u>holy</u> city of Mecca in the country now known as Saudi Arabia. I had wanted to go on the *hajj* for a long time, and I was looking forward to the journey. However, at the same time I felt sad about leaving my family and friends, especially my parents. I knew that I would be away on the *hajj* for only 16 months, but I *didn't* know that it would be 24 years before I returned to Tangier.

Unfortunately, I hadn't been able to find a group of people to travel with, so I had to set off by myself. Travelling alone was very dangerous, as you could be attacked by thieves and sometimes even killed. It was much safer to journey in a group, so, when it was possible, I preferred to join a caravan, a group of people travelling in the same direction. My route was along the North African coast through Tunis, and then to the historical city of Alexandria, where I arrived in April 1326. There I saw the famous lighthouse, one of the seven wonders of the ancient world. I also met a holy man who <u>inspired</u> me with the idea of travelling to India and China.

From Alexandria, I travelled to the beautiful city of Cairo and saw the great River Nile, then I travelled east into Syria. I was very <u>impressed</u> by the <u>magnificent</u> Ummayed <u>Mosque</u> in Damascus. After spending the holy month of Ramadan in Damascus, I joined a large caravan of <u>pilgrims</u> travelling south on the journey they made every year to the cities of Medina and Mecca. The journey between Syria and Medina was very difficult as we had to cross the desert. We travelled as quickly as possible by day and night in order to get safely to the other side. At last we reached Mecca, where I received a very kind and friendly welcome from the people.

◆ ◆ ◆

I'd succeeded in travelling to Mecca for the *hajj*, but I wasn't keen to return to Morocco. I wanted to do more travelling, and see more new places. So on 17th November 1326, I joined a caravan of pilgrims from Iraq who were travelling home across Arabia. We journeyed north to Medina, and then on to Najaf in Iraq, travelling mainly at night because it was cooler.

At Najaf, I left the caravan and went south to Basra, before returning north across the mountains to the great trading city of Baghdad. I arrived in Baghdad in 1327, where I was surprised by the large number of bathhouses, places where people could wash and have baths, and by the wonderful markets.

I found a large group of Mongols who were travelling north, and I joined them for a while. Then I left them and travelled east to the Persian city of Tabriz. Tabriz was on the Silk Road, so it was an important centre for trade. It had a wonderful market where I saw many magnificent jewels. My plan was to return to Mecca for another *hajj*, and I set off on the long journey south. But the journey across the Arabian desert was difficult and tiring, and I became very ill. By the time I arrived in Mecca, I was completely weak and exhausted. I stayed there until I felt strong enough to travel again, then I set out for the port of Jeddah on the Red Sea coast in the country now known as Saudi Arabia.

From Jeddah I took a boat south to Yemen, sailing slowly along the coast. This was my first voyage, and I found it very unpleasant. The winds were strong, the seas were rough with high waves, and many passengers became ill. At last, we reached Yemen, from where we sailed to Somalia, arriving in 1331 in the city of Mogadishu. Like Baghdad, Mogadishu was a great trading centre. However, I didn't stay there long, but continued on to Mombasa and then to other places in Africa. After returning to Mecca for the *hajj* again, I joined a caravan which was going to Anatolia in eastern Turkey. I had a new and ambitious plan. I was hoping to join a caravan in Anatolia which was travelling to India, because I wanted to find work with the Sultan of Delhi.

◆ ◆ ◆

I arrived in Alanya, on the southern coast of Turkey, and from there I travelled by land to Konya in central Turkey, then north to Sinope on the Black Sea coast. Eventually I arrived in the city of Constantinople (now Istanbul). This was the first time I had stayed in a city that wasn't Muslim. The Greek influence in Constantinople was very strong, and the people had a very different way of life from Islam. After a month in Constantinople, I travelled to Bukhara and Samarkand, then I journeyed south to Afghanistan. Finally I crossed into India through the mountains of the Hindu Kush, and continued on to Delhi, where I met Sultan Muhammad bin Tughluq.

Muhammad bin Tughluq was a Muslim, and he was famous as the wealthiest man in the Muslim world. He was very interested in me because I knew about Islamic law, and he <u>appointed</u> me as a *qadi,* a judge. Unfortunately, there were millions of poor people living outside the Sultan's <u>court</u> who didn't care about Islamic law, and who didn't respect my opinions and <u>judgments</u>. I worked for the Sultan for six years, but my job was sometimes very difficult because the Sultan's moods kept changing. Sometimes he listened to me with respect, but at other times he behaved as if I was a traitor, an enemy of his country. At those times I was afraid that my life was in danger.

For that reason, I was very keen to get away from the Sultan's court. However, I needed a good excuse to leave, so I told him that I wanted to go on another *hajj*. But the Sultan had other plans for me, and asked me to go to China as his <u>ambassador</u> to the Emperor, the head of the Chinese <u>Empire</u>. I was very interested in this opportunity to visit a new country, so I agreed to go. However, as I was travelling to the coast to find a ship for China, a terrible thing happened. Our group was attacked by thieves, who stole my money and nearly killed me. I became separated from the other travellers, but ten days later, I managed to find them again and we <u>set sail</u> in two ships for Calicut in southern India.

But here we had another <u>disaster</u>. I went <u>ashore</u> to visit a mosque in Kozhikode, but while I was away from my ship, there was a terrible storm. My ship sank and the other ship sailed away without me, leaving me <u>stranded</u>. I was afraid to return to Delhi because I knew that the Sultan would be angry with me – I'd not only lost one of his ships, but I'd lost a lot of money too. So I decided to travel on to China, and take up my position as ambassador, visiting the Maldive Islands on the way. The people of the Maldives had been Buddhists but they'd recently changed their religion to Islam. So they were very interested to learn about my skills in Islamic law, and they appointed me as Chief Judge.

However, the Maldive people considered that some of my judgments were too strict. In addition, I didn't approve of some things about their way of life, but when I complained about these things, nobody listened to me. So finally I left the Maldives and set sail for Sri Lanka, but there was a disaster when my ship sank near the coast. Another ship came to rescue us, but this ship was attacked by <u>pirates</u>, and again I was left stranded on the <u>shore</u>. At last I arrived back in the Maldives and found a ship heading for China. We sailed to the country now known as Bangladesh, and then to a number of other countries in the Far East before arriving in Quanzhou in Fujian, China.

I saw many amazing things in China and was greatly impressed by them. The artists there were very <u>skilful</u>, and made beautiful things out of <u>silk</u> and <u>porcelain</u>. The Chinese people used a system that I had never seen before – they used paper money to <u>trade</u>. I visited many places, including Hangzhou, a very attractive city, which was situated around a beautiful lake and surrounded by green hills. It was one of the largest cities I'd ever seen! I was also impressed by the wooden Chinese ships, which were very well made and beautifully decorated with coloured sails and silk. After leaving Hangzhou, I travelled to Beijing, and was invited to the magnificent court of the Emperor, where I had more wonderful experiences.

However, after all my years away from home, I felt it was time for me to return to Morocco. So I left China, and in 1348, after more adventures, I eventually arrived in Damascus. But I found Damascus greatly changed. A terrible disease called the Black Death was spreading quickly through the city, and thousands of people were dying. Everyone was afraid of the Black Death because there was no cure. If you caught it, you usually died very quickly. So I decided to leave for another *hajj* to Mecca, before returning to Morocco. In 1349, I finally arrived in Tangier, the city of my birth, but my return was sad because, on the way, I'd received news that my parents had died.

◆ ◆ ◆

I crossed the sea to Iberia, then came back and travelled around Morocco. Now I had another ambitious plan – to cross the Sahara Desert and visit the Muslim countries on the other side. So I travelled to the northern edge of the desert, where I bought <u>camels</u> and food. In February 1352, I joined a caravan, which included several <u>merchants</u>. We set off across the Sahara, and after 25 days we arrived at the village of Taqhaza. There was something very unusual about Taqhaza – salt! There was a salt mine in the sand nearby, and all the houses were made from huge blocks of salt, with camel skins for roofs. The local people used salt for trading, just like gold and silver.

Our journey across the Sahara took two months, and during this time we crossed 1,600 kilometres of desert. You had to stay with the caravan, because if you got separated from it, you couldn't survive alone in the desert. Sometimes we came across the bodies of travellers who had got lost, and died from heat and lack of water. After reaching the other side of the Sahara, I travelled along a river which I thought was the River Nile (although actually it was the River Niger). I reached the city of Mali, the capital of the Mali <u>Empire</u>,

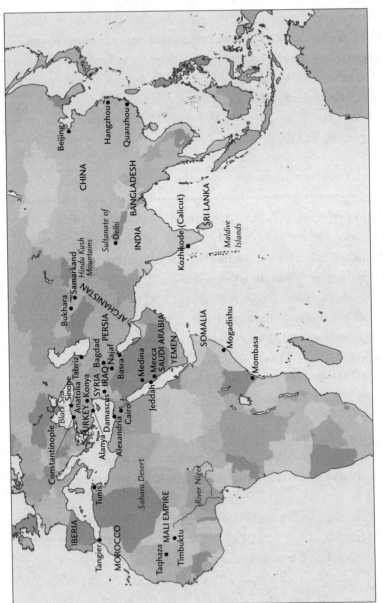

Countries and cities visited by Ibn Battuta

where the King and his people welcomed me. Although they behaved to me with respect, I found some of their traditions very strange. In addition, I wasn't used to their food, and I often became ill.

After eight months, I left Mali with a merchant called Abu Bakr, and journeyed by land to Timbuktu. On the way, we came to a wide river which we had to cross by boat. I saw sixteen huge creatures entering the water, and I thought they must be elephants. But when I asked Abu Bakr about them, he told me they were <u>hippopotamuses</u>. I had never seen such strange creatures before! After staying in Timbuktu for a short time, I journeyed down the River Niger, and then back across the desert. However, on the way, I received a message from the Sultan of Morocco, ordering me to come home at once. So I travelled back to Morocco, arriving there in early 1354.

That was the end of my travels, and I stayed in Morocco until my death around 1369. The Sultan appointed me as a *qadi*, and I became very friendly with him. He enjoyed hearing about my adventures, and he asked me to write them all down. So I told my stories to Ibn Juzayy, a scholar I'd met on my travels, and he wrote everything down in a book called *Rihla Ibn Battuta* (Ibn Battuta's Travels). I am remembered now not only because I was a great traveller, but because I described everything I saw in the 44 countries that I visited. Some people didn't believe I visited as many countries as I said I did, but this is the story of my life as I told it. When people read my book, they can learn many interesting things about the world in my time.

The Life of Abu Abdullah
Muhammad Ibn Battuta

1304   Abu Abdullah Muhammad Ibn Battuta, usually known as Ibn Battuta, was born into a family of scholars in Islamic law, in Tangier, Morocco.

1325   Aged 21, he left home alone to go on a *hajj* (pilgrimage) to Mecca. He travelled across North Africa to Egypt, visiting Palestine and Syria along the way, then down to Medina and Mecca.

1326–1328   Ibn Battuta arrived in Mecca but decided to continue travelling. He journeyed through Iraq and Persia, then returned to Mecca and stayed there for a year.

1328–1333   He sailed from Jeddah to Yemen then to East Africa. He travelled through the Middle East and Turkey, before joining a caravan to India.

1334–1341   He reached India and was welcomed by the Sultan of Delhi, who made him a *qadi*, a Muslim judge. Later, the Sultan offered him the post of ambassador to the Emperor of China.

1342–1346   Ibn Battuta set sail for China, but became stranded in India. He went to the Maldive Islands, where he was appointed as Chief Judge. He travelled to Sri Lanka, Bangladesh and countries in the Far East, eventually reaching China.

1346–1348   He returned home via India and the Middle East. On the way, he found that the Black Death had started in Damascus. He went on another *hajj* to Mecca.

1349–1351   He arrived back in Tangier, Morocco. Sadly, during his travels his parents had died. He crossed the Strait of Gibraltar to Iberia.

1352–1353   He joined a desert caravan and travelled across the Sahara Desert to the city of Mali in the West African Empire of Mali.

1354–1355   The Sultan of Morocco ordered Ibn Battuta to return, and appointed him a judge. Ibn Juzayy, a scholar, wrote down Ibn Battuta's stories in *Rihla Ibn Battuta* (Travels of Ibn Battuta).

*c.*1369   After travelling over 120,000 kilometres and visiting 44 countries, Ibn Battuta died in Morocco at around the age of 64.

Christopher Columbus

◆ ◆ ◆

1451–1506

the man who discovered new worlds

I was one of the most famous explorers in history. Although I didn't discover America, as some people believe, I opened up new worlds to Europeans. I was an expert sailor and <u>navigator</u>, who made four <u>voyages</u> across the Atlantic.

◆ ◆ ◆

I was born in Genoa, on the north-west coast of Italy, in 1451. From an early age, I loved the sea, and I made my first voyage when I was only ten years old. In 1473, I <u>became apprenticed to</u> one of the most important families in Genoa, the Centurione family. I sailed on several trading voyages for the family, buying and selling <u>goods</u>, but in 1476, a <u>disaster</u> happened which nearly ended my life. My <u>fleet</u> was attacked near the coast of Portugal by French privateers, ships carrying weapons whose owners were paid by the French government to attack enemy ships. My ship was destroyed, but fortunately I was able to swim <u>ashore</u>.

I travelled to Lisbon, where my brother Bartholemew had a job making maps. After that, I continued working for the Centurione family. I made several more voyages, buying and selling goods in England, Ireland and Iceland, as well as in Guinea on the west coast of Africa. I married into a rich family; my wife's name was Filipa Moniz Perestrelo, and she was the daughter of the Governor of Porto Santo, who'd been a navigator and explorer. Filipa gave me charts of the Atlantic Ocean which her father had drawn, and these maps were very helpful to me. In 1480, we had a son who we named Diego Colón, but sadly, Filipa died in 1485 and Diego and I moved to Cadiz in Spain.

By 1488, I was busy making plans for an <u>ambitious</u> voyage – to discover a sea route to China and India. These countries in the East were sources of valuable goods such as <u>silk</u> and <u>spices</u>, which people in Europe wanted. These goods were brought to Europe by <u>merchants</u> travelling along the <u>Silk Road</u>. This journey passed through many countries and was very difficult and dangerous. However, I was sure it would be possible to travel *west* by sea around the world to reach the countries of the East. In 1483 I spoke to the King of Portugal, and asked him to sponsor me – in other words, to give me money to buy ships and men for my voyage. But I was very disappointed when he refused to support me.

◆ ◆ ◆

The First Voyage (1492–1493)

Next, I spoke to King Ferdinand and Queen Isabella of Spain. I promised them that if they gave me money for my voyage,

I'd bring back great wealth for Spain from the countries in the East. It wasn't easy to persuade them, especially as my ideas about the size of the Earth and the oceans were different from other people's. Many people laughed at me, and said I was a fool, and that my ships would fall off the end of the world. But at last the King and Queen agreed to support me. I knew the journey would be dangerous, but I found some brave sailors who were looking for <u>adventure</u> and the chance to become rich. On 3rd August 1492, I <u>set sail</u> from Palos in Spain with three ships and a crew of 90 sailors.

Our flagship, the largest ship, was named the *Santa Maria*, and the two smaller ships were the *Pinta* and the *Niña*. After stopping for a month for repair work at Gomera in the Canary Islands, we sailed across the Atlantic for 35 days. But then we <u>ran into</u> some serious problems because we'd eaten almost all our food. The crew became worried and unhappy, and said that they would no longer do what I told them. They said that if I didn't turn the ship around, they'd throw me into the sea! Fortunately, the next day, 11th October, we saw land, and I was convinced that we'd reached India.

On 12th October 1492 we landed on an island which we <u>claimed</u> immediately for Spain and named San Salvador. The <u>native</u> island people were friendly, and I noticed that they were wearing jewellery made of gold. From there we sailed to another island, which I called Juana (it's now called Cuba), and then east to an island which we named Hispaniola, now made up of Haiti and the Dominican Republic. However, on Christmas Day, 1492, a terrible accident happened. Our flagship, the *Santa Maria*, hit the rocks near the coast of Hispaniola, broke into pieces, and sank. With the help of the island people, we rescued everything we could from our broken ship and used it to build a settlement, *Villa de la Navidad* (Christmas Town).

Unfortunately, there was no room for the 39 sailors of the *Santa Maria's* crew in the two smaller ships, so I had to leave them behind on Hispaniola. After promising that I'd return for them as quickly as I could, I set sail for Spain on 16th January with the *Pinta* and the *Niña*. But the voyage across the sea in winter was very dangerous, with storms and huge waves. Our two ships became separated and we were forced to stop at Lisbon in Portugal. The *Niña* arrived there on 3rd March 1493, and the *Pinta* on 15th March. A week later, I reached Spain, where there were great celebrations at my return. King Ferdinand and Queen Isabella were delighted when I told them I'd found a route across the sea to India and China, and they gave me a new title – Governor of the Indies.

◆ ◆ ◆

The Second Voyage (1493–1496)

My first voyage hadn't been completely successful; I'd returned to Spain having lost my best ship, and without much gold. So I persuaded King Ferdinand and Queen Isabella that I needed to go back and continue searching for China and Japan. I was sure that those countries were near the islands which I'd already discovered. So in September 1493, I set sail again, but this time with a much larger fleet of 17 ships and over a thousand men. My orders from the King and Queen were to increase the size of the settlement on Hispaniola and <u>establish</u> <u>trade</u> routes with the cities of the Far East. We crossed the Atlantic quickly, and on 22nd November we reached Hispaniola.

But on Hispaniola we found a terrible situation. All the 39 sailors I had left behind were dead. I was told that the island people had become angry because my men had taken some women from a local <u>tribe</u>, and so they'd killed them. We had to leave that place, but I started a new settlement on the north coast of Hispaniola, which we called La Isabella, the name of the Queen of Spain. We also started exploring other parts of the island to look for gold, but we didn't find much. So in April 1494 I took three ships and went to look for China, but instead we landed on Juana (Cuba). I was convinced that Juana was part of China, and not an island! From Juana we sailed to Jamaica, but the people were unfriendly, so we returned to Hispaniola.

I was an excellent sea captain, but I didn't do very well as governor of Hispaniola and the Indies. Some of the young Spaniards who sailed with me refused to accept my <u>authority</u>, because they thought of me as an Italian foreigner. In addition, many of the native Indian tribes were very unfriendly. They kept attacking us, but we defeated them. I sent a letter to Queen Isabella, telling her that I planned to take some of the island people as <u>slaves</u>, and sell them. But she wasn't happy about that idea, and ordered me not to do it. On 10th March 1496, I set sail for Spain, leaving my brothers to govern the settlement.

◆ ◆ ◆

The Third Voyage (1498–1500)

On 30th May 1498, I set sail once more from Spain on another trip to the <u>New World</u>, this time with a fleet of six ships. Three ships sailed to Hispaniola, carrying fresh supplies of food to the people in the settlement, while I led the other three ships south to do more exploring. Unfortunately, in the middle of the Atlantic, we ran into the doldrums, which are an area with no wind, so that our ships couldn't move for several days. Just as our water supplies were getting dangerously low, the winds started blowing again. We sailed on, until an island with three hills appeared, which I called Trinidad. On 31st July, we landed our ships on the southern coast of this island, where we got fresh supplies of food and water.

From Trinidad we explored the Gulf of Paria, which separates Trinidad from the country now called Venezuela, near the mouth of the great Orinoco River. We landed on the coast of South America, and so we became the first Europeans to arrive in this great land. However, by this time I was becoming seriously ill, so I decided that we would return to Hispaniola. But when we reached the island on 19th August, we found an awful situation. Many of the settlers who'd come from Spain were refusing to accept my authority. They said that I'd lied about the wealth of the New World, and they complained about how my two brothers were governing the settlement.

But there was something worse. Many of the settlers and sailors who'd returned from Hispaniola to Spain had complained about me to King Ferdinand and Queen Isabella. As a result, in 1500 the King and Queen sent a royal <u>official</u>, Francisco de Bobadilla, to Hispaniola with orders to remove me from power. My brothers and I were arrested and sent back to Spain in chains. We were put in prison, but after several weeks, we were freed and I was allowed to return to the New World. However, I'd lost my title of Governor of the Indies, and Bobadilla had become Governor in my place.

♦ ♦ ♦

The Fourth Voyage (1502–1504)

I persuaded the King and Queen to allow me to go on one last voyage to find the wealth I'd promised them. In addition, I still wanted to find the route across the sea to the Indian Ocean. So on 11th May 1502, I left Cadiz in Spain with three ships and 140 men, including my brother, Bartholemew. But when we reached Hispaniola, the new governor, Bobadilla, wouldn't let me land. The seas were very rough and dangerous, and I knew there was going to be a hurricane – a storm with very strong winds. I warned Bobadilla, but he wouldn't listen to me. Against my advice, a Spanish fleet of 30 ships left the island carrying a large amount of gold, while my own ships were safe at the mouth of the River Jaina.

As a result, my ships had only a little damage, but Bobadilla's fleet sailed straight into the hurricane, and 29 of his 30 ships sank. 500 men died, including Bobadilla, and all the gold was lost. After this disaster, we left Hispaniola and spent the next two months exploring Central America, arriving in Panama on 16th October 1502. In January 1503, I left a group of soldiers to guard the mouth of the Belén River. But on 6th April, one of our ships became <u>stranded</u> in the river and couldn't move, and our soldiers were attacked by native tribes. So on 16th April we left Panama and went north. However, we ran into a storm near the coast of Cuba, and on 25th June 1503 we became stranded in St. Ann's Bay, Jamaica.

We stayed stranded on Jamaica for a whole year in difficult conditions. The native tribes there weren't happy about us being on their island, and, after some months, they didn't want to give us any more food. Luckily, I had an <u>astronomical</u> chart, and I found out that on 29th February 1504, there was going to be an eclipse of the Moon, a very unusual event when the Earth passes between the Sun and the Moon. I told the island people that the Moon was going to grow dark, but they didn't believe me. When it happened, they were so <u>impressed</u> that they continued giving us food. Ships finally

The Voyages of Christopher Columbus

Legend:
- 1st Voyage ············
- 2nd Voyage — — —
- 3rd Voyage ———
- 4th Voyage – – – –

Labels: NORTH AMERICA, MEXICO, Gulf of Mexico, CUBA, HONDURAS, NICARAGUA, COSTA RICA, PANAMA, Belén River, Caribbean Sea, VENEZUELA, COLOMBIA, Orinoco River, BRAZIL, Amazon River, Pacific Ocean, Atlantic Ocean, Sargasso Sea, Canary Islands, PORTUGAL, SPAIN, Lisbon, Palos, Cadiz, AFRICA, Niger River arrived to help us in June, and my men and I sailed back to Spain, arriving there on 7th November 1504.

My fourth voyage was my final one. I'd been suffering from serious illnesses for many years, and I knew I didn't have much longer to live. I died in Spain on 20th May 1506. When I thought about my life, I knew that I'd brought about some important changes. I'd opened up the New World to Europe, established settlements there, and brought back wealth for Spain. Many countries in the New World still celebrate the anniversary of my arrival in the Americas on 12th October 1492, as an official holiday. Although it's celebrated as Columbus Day in the United States, it has different names in Spain and Latin American countries.

The Life of Christopher Columbus

1451   Christopher Columbus was born in Genoa,
        Italy.

1461   At the age of ten, Christopher made his
        first sea voyage.

1470   Christopher moved to Savona with his
        family. He travelled the sea as a privateer
        and attacked ships belonging to the Moors.

1473   He became an <u>apprentice</u> to the
        Centurione family.

1476   He made trading voyages to England,
        Ireland and Iceland. His ship sank in an
        attack near Portugal and he swam ashore.

1477   He joined his brother, Bartholomew,
        who had a job making maps in Lisbon.
        He continued to <u>trade</u> for the Centurione
        family.

1479   Christopher married into a rich family. His
        wife, Filipa Moniz Perestrelo, gave him her
        father's charts of the Atlantic Ocean.

1480   Filipa and Christopher had a son, Diego
        Colón.

1482   Christopher spent the next few years
        trading along the coasts of West Africa.

1484–1485	Filipa died and Christopher took his son to live in Cadiz in Spain, and opened a shop selling maps and charts.
1487	Christopher tried to persuade King Ferdinand and Queen Isabella of Spain to sponsor his voyage.
1492	Ferdinand and Isabella agreed to sponsor Christopher and provide money and ships. His first voyage was from August 1492 to March 1493. He established the first Spanish settlement in the New World.
1493–1496	Christopher's second voyage lasted from September 1493 to June 1496. He established another Spanish settlement.
1498–1500	His third voyage lasted from May 1498 to October 1500. He became the first European to land in South America.
1502–1504	His fourth voyage lasted from May 1502 to late 1504. He discovered Guanaja Island and Honduras in Central America.
1506	Christopher died from an illness in Valladolid, Spain, on 20th May 1506, aged 54.

James Cook

◆ ◆ ◆

1728–1779

the first man to sail around the world in
both directions

**I was the first European to discover Australia. I was very
<u>skilful</u> at navigating and making maps. I was the first man
to sail around the world in both directions. But I also
understood the needs of ordinary sailors.**

♦ ◆ ♦

I was born in the village of Marton in Yorkshire, England,
the second of eight children. In 1736, my father got a job
as manager on a farm in the village of Great Ayton, and
after leaving school at the age of 13, I helped him with that
work. But I wasn't good at farm work, so in 1745, I <u>became
apprenticed to</u> Mr Sanderson, the owner of a shop in the
fishing village of Staithes, 20 miles away. However, he soon
realized that I was more interested in the sea than in his shop!
So he took me to the port of Whitby and introduced me to
his friends, John and Henry Walker, who were local ship
owners. They accepted me as their <u>apprentice</u>, and for the
next three years, I sailed on ships carrying coal between the
River Tyne in the north of England, and London.

During my years as an apprentice, from 1746 to 1749, I learned valuable sailing skills, as well as mathematics, astronomy and navigation. In 1749, I started working on trading ships in the Baltic Sea, but then, in 1755, a new chapter of my life began. Britain was preparing for a war against France and Spain, later called the Seven Years' War. I was very keen to serve my king and country, so I joined the British Royal Navy. Soon, I was taking part in sea battles against the French navy. My first post was on a ship called *HMS Eagle*. In November 1755, I helped to take a French warship prisoner, and sink another. In June 1757, I passed my Master's examinations, which meant that I was now qualified to navigate a sailing ship.

After a short time on *HMS Solebay*, I got a post as Master on *HMS Pembroke* and sailed across the Atlantic to defend the British lands in Canada against the French. I was taught surveying and map-making by an expert surveyor, Samuel Holland, and I became very skilful at this work. The Canadian winters were freezing cold, and it was impossible for our ships to move because the sea was blocked with ice. During these periods when we couldn't sail anywhere, Samuel Holland and I drew maps of the Gulf of St Lawrence and the entrance to the St Lawrence River. Later in the 1760s, I was able to use my skills in surveying and map-making to draw detailed maps of the coast of Newfoundland.

◆ ◆ ◆

When I joined the Royal Navy in 1755, I'd stayed at a small hotel in Wapping in East London, called the Bell Inn. The owner and his wife were called Mr and Mrs Batts, and they had a young daughter, Elizabeth. During the next few years, when I was home from the Navy, I went back to Wapping and stayed at the Bell Inn. By 1762, Elizabeth had grown up into a beautiful young lady. Although I was 34 and she was 21, we fell in love, and I asked her to marry me. In spite of the difference in our ages, she agreed, and we were married on 21st December 1762 with great celebrations. Before I went to sea again, I bought a house for us. Although I was away on my voyages for much of our married life, we had six children.

The Seven Years' War ended and the Navy sent me back to Canada in May 1763. My job was to make maps of the coast of the island of Newfoundland and the Gulf of St Lawrence. During the next few years, I spent six months of each year surveying and making maps in Canada. When the freezing Canadian winters started, and the seas were blocked by ice, I returned to England. My maps were the first accurate and detailed maps of the areas round Newfoundland, and they were noticed by the members of the Royal Society. This was an organization of scientists whose aim was to increase scientific discoveries in the world. The members were very impressed by my maps and greatly admired my skills in surveying and making maps.

From the start of my career, I'd learned about astronomy, and in 1766, I reported on an eclipse of the Sun in Newfoundland, a very unusual event when the Moon passes between the Earth and the Sun. This impressed the Royal Society's members even more, as they were planning an expedition which involved astronomy. In 1769, the planet Venus was going to pass in front of the Sun. The scientists in the Royal Society had decided that the best place to watch this event would be the island of Tahiti in the South Pacific Ocean. They were looking for a captain to lead an expedition there and record the passing of Venus. This information would help astronomers to decide the distance between the Earth and the Sun. I was very interested in the expedition, so I accepted the job.

◆ ◆ ◆

The First Voyage (1768–1771)

In August 1768, I set sail from Plymouth in the west of England on a ship called *HMS Endeavour*. Having travelled west across the Atlantic to Rio de Janeiro, we sailed on to Tahiti, landing there in April 1769. We established a camp, and stayed there for the next three months, successfully measuring and recording the passing of Venus. The official purpose of the expedition had been to find out information for the Royal Society. However, I'd also received secret orders from the Admiralty, the headquarters of the Royal Navy, to continue our voyage. At that time, people believed that there was a southern continent, a huge area of land, which they called Terra Australis. I was ordered to find this continent, and claim it for Britain.

We sailed west across the Pacific, and reached the islands of New Zealand. Having sailed around the two large islands, and some smaller ones, I mapped them in great detail and claimed them for Britain. Next, we headed west to the land known as New Holland, which no Englishman had visited before. On 29th April 1770, we landed in a bay which at first we called Stingray Harbour. We called it that because of the large number of stingrays, a kind of huge flat fish, which we saw there. However, I'd brought two botanists, scientists who studied plants, on the voyage. They found so many new and wonderful kinds of plants around the bay that we changed its name to Botany Bay. We also came across the native people of the land, the Aborigines.

We named the area New South Wales (now a state of Australia), then we sailed north up the coast. We found land that had never been seen by Europeans before, and I made detailed maps of that coast. However, we ran into terrible danger when we hit the Great Barrier Reef. Water flooded into *HMS Endeavour* and badly damaged the ship. We were forced to spend two months on shore while we repaired it. However, during that time we found all sorts of interesting animals and plants, including kangaroos. In August 1770, we started the long journey home, sailing to the island of Batavia (now known as Jakarta in Indonesia), then across the Indian Ocean and round the point of southern Africa at the Cape of Good Hope. We finally reached Britain on 12th July 1771.

It was wonderful to be home and see Elizabeth again, although I'd been away for such a long time that my children didn't recognize me! Elizabeth had had a baby, Joseph, just after I left in 1768, but sadly, he only lived for a month. Although we'd discovered many new things on our voyage, the trip had been long and dangerous, and many of my crew had died. I was always worried about the health of my men. I was strict about keeping my ship clean, and I made sure my crew had plenty of fresh food. I knew that fruit was important, because it helped to stop the men becoming ill with scurvy. Scurvy was a disease common among sailors, which they got because they didn't have enough Vitamin C. My men hadn't died from scurvy, but when we went <u>ashore</u> at Batavia, over 30 of them had died from malaria, a disease carried by <u>mosquitoes</u>.

◆ ◆ ◆

The Second Voyage (1772–1775)

In August 1771, shortly after my return, I was <u>promoted</u> to Commander. Then in 1772, the Admiralty decided to send me on another expedition, with the aim of either finding the continent of Terra Australis, or proving that it didn't exist. On my first voyage, I'd sailed all around the islands of New Zealand, proving that they weren't part of a continent. In addition, I'd charted the east coast of Australia, discovering that Australia was a huge area of land. But some scientists in the Royal Society were still convinced that the continent of Terra Australis was further south. So, I set off with two ships: *HMS Resolution* and *HMS Adventure*. I commanded *HMS Resolution* and *HMS Adventure* was commanded by Captain Furneaux.

On 17th January 1773, we became probably the first ships to cross the Antarctic Circle. But we ran into terrible weather, and our two ships became separated. Captain Furneaux went north to New Zealand, and I continued exploring the dangerous waters of the Antarctic. But I didn't find a continent because I had to sail north to Tahiti to get fresh supplies of food and other things. I tried again to find Terra Australis, but I couldn't. After returning to New Zealand in 1774, our ships set sail for home. We took a young man

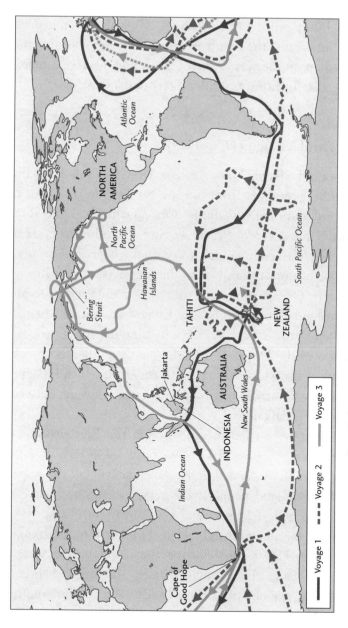

Captain James Cook's Voyages through the South Pacific

——— Voyage 1   – – – Voyage 2   ——— Voyage 3

from Tahiti called Omai with us. We sailed around Cape Horn and across the South Atlantic, claiming several islands for Britain on the way. When I got home, I wrote a report, saying that Terra Australis definitely didn't exist.

◆ ◆ ◆

The Third Voyage (1776–1779)

Although the Royal Navy had asked me if I wanted to retire, I couldn't stay away from the sea. So in 1776, I set out on my third and final expedition. Once again I had two ships: I commanded *HMS Resolution*, and the other ship, *HMS Discovery*, was commanded by Captain Clerke. The main purpose of our voyage was to discover a sea route through the Arctic Ocean connecting the Atlantic and Pacific Oceans. First we sailed to Tahiti to take Omai back home. Then we travelled north, and in 1778 we became the first Europeans to discover the Hawaiian Islands. We then sailed north-east to explore the west coast of North America, which I mapped all the way to the Bering Strait, the channel of water between Russia and Alaska.

Although we tried to sail through the Bering Strait, it was blocked by ice, so in 1779, we returned to Hawaii. After a few weeks, we landed at Kealakekua Bay on the largest island. The island people were very friendly, and some of them even believed that I was a god! A month later, we set sail again, but unfortunately we had to return to Kealakekua for repairs. However, this time the island people weren't pleased to see us. They fought with us, and on 14th February 1779, they stole one of our small boats. We got into another boat and followed them ashore. We were planning to take their king as our prisoner and keep him until our missing boat was given back. But we didn't succeed, so we had to return to the beach.

As I was helping my men to push our boat into the sea, I was hit on the head. I fell on my face in the water, and the island people killed me with a knife. They took my body away, but later they gave back some parts of it to my crew so that I could be buried at sea. My ships returned to England in October 1780, and a report about my third voyage was given to King George the Third. People were very sad about my death, as they thought of me as a national hero. I'd sailed into unknown regions, discovering and mapping the coasts of new countries. In addition, I'd taken artists and scientists with me, who'd drawn pictures of the places we visited, and collected information about plants and animals. As a result of my voyages, people learned new things about the world.

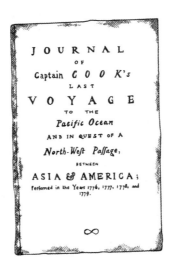

The Life of James Cook

1728   James Cook was born in Marton, Yorkshire, England.

1736   His family moved to Aireyholme Farm at Great Ayton, where his father worked as farm manager.

1745–1746   James became an apprentice in a shop in the fishing village of Staithes. He moved to Whitby and became apprenticed to ship owners, John and Henry Walker.

1749   After completing his training, James started working on trading ships to the Baltic.

1755–1757   He joined the Royal Navy at Wapping, London. He served as Master's assistant on *HMS Eagle*, then joined *HMS Solebay* before becoming Master of *HMS Pembroke*. During the Seven Years' War, he helped to survey and map the St Lawrence River in Canada.

1762–1767   James returned to England and married Elizabeth Batts. They later had six children. The Admiralty gave him the job of surveying the coasts of Newfoundland and Labrador, on *HMS Grenville*. In 1766, he noted an eclipse of the Sun in Newfoundland.

1768–1771   The First Voyage, on *HMS Endeavour*.
James was asked by the members of the
Royal Society to watch and report on
the passing of Venus in front of the Sun.
He was also ordered to find the southern
continent of Terra Australis. He mapped
the islands of New Zealand, and the coasts
of New South Wales and east Australia.

1772–1775   The Second Voyage, with two ships:
HMS Resolution and *HMS Adventure*. The
purpose was to continue searching for Terra
Australis. James crossed the Antarctic Circle
and sailed round Antarctica, discovering
many islands in the South Pacific.

1775   James returned to England, and was made
a Fellow of the Royal Society. He also
received the Copley Gold Medal. He
became the first man in history to have
sailed around the world in both directions.

1776–1779   The Third Voyage, with two ships:
HMS Resolution and *HMS Discovery*. The
purpose was to discover the Northwest
Passage. After sailing to Tahiti, he mapped
the north-west American coast, before
returning to Hawaii.

1779   During a fight between James' men
and Hawaiian native island people at
Kealakekua Bay on 14th February, James
was attacked and killed.

David Livingstone

• ◆ •

1813–1873

the man who explored Africa

I was one of the most famous explorers and <u>pioneers</u> of Africa. I was the first European to discover the Zambezi River and the Victoria Falls. I survived many dangers, and did my best to stop the African <u>slave</u> <u>trade</u>.

◆ ◆ ◆

I was born in Blantyre, in South Lanarkshire in Scotland, on 19th March 1813. I was the second of seven children. My family was poor, so very early in my life, I learned what hard work was like. When I was ten, I started working in the local cotton <u>mill</u> to earn money for my family. I stayed there for the next 16 years. However, the mill owner believed that children's education was important too. So although I was working at the mill for 12 hours every day, I attended school lessons in the evenings and at weekends, and learned to read and write. My parents were Christians, and sometimes Christian <u>preachers</u> visited our area to give talks. Some of these preachers <u>inspired</u> me to travel to other countries to work as a Christian <u>missionary</u>.

My dream was to become a missionary doctor, but first I had to become qualified in medicine. In 1836, I began studying medicine and theology, the study of religion, at Anderson's College (now the University of Strathclyde) and Glasgow University. I had heard about the London Missionary Society (LMS), an organization whose purpose was to spread Christianity to other countries. I applied to join it, and I was delighted when I was accepted. First I had to finish my missionary training. A door to wonderful new opportunities was now open to me! I'd been planning to work in China, but in September 1839, a war had started there, so the LMS suggested that I should go to work in the West Indies instead.

However, in 1840 I met a man who changed my life. He was Robert Moffat, a Scottish missionary, who was visiting the LMS from Kuruman, a missionary <u>outpost</u> in the southern part of Africa. This outpost, the place where the missionaries worked, was in the African countryside, north of the Orange River. I was very excited by Moffat's descriptions of Africa and his work. At one of his talks, he said, 'I have sometimes seen, in the morning sun, the smoke of a thousand villages where no missionary has ever been.' How wonderful it would be, I thought, to go to such a place! Robert Moffat encouraged me in my dream to go to Africa, and I became convinced that my future was in Africa.

◆ ◆ ◆

I was sure that I had a calling, a special duty, to go and work in Kuruman. So in 1841, I arrived at the missionary

outpost there after a long and difficult journey. However, I wanted to <u>preach</u> Christianity in other places as well, so in 1844, I went further north to start a new missionary outpost at Mabotswa. I built a house there, and travelled around the small villages in a cart pulled by <u>oxen</u>. When the people in the village learned that a doctor was coming, crowds of sick people would surround my <u>ox</u>-cart and ask me for help. However, one day, I had a very frightening experience. I was attacked by a lion, which caught me by the shoulder and shook me. Although I was saved by a local teacher, Mebalwe, I suffered from terrible pain in my arm for the rest of my life.

While my arm was getting better, I travelled back to Kuruman to visit Robert Moffat. There I met his daughter, Mary, and we fell in love. We got married in January 1845. Mary was a great help to me, sharing my work of preaching Christianity and teaching the local children. She'd lived in Africa from a very young age, and spoke the local Setswana language. Over the next years, we had six children, although sadly, one daughter, Elizabeth, died two months after her birth. Mary and the children often came with me on my journeys, although this made me very worried when the children became ill from disease. In 1849 and 1851, we made two trips across the Kalahari Desert, and on the second trip, I saw the upper part of the great Zambezi River.

I very much wanted to explore more of Africa, but I was worried about Mary and the children. I realized that it was dangerous for them to continue coming with me on my journeys, so in 1852, I decided to send them back to England. Although I missed them very much, I knew that I had to carry on exploring Africa by myself. In 1855, I became the first European to discover a <u>magnificent</u> waterfall. It was called 'the smoke that thunders' in the local language, but I named it the Victoria Falls because our British queen's name was Victoria. In May 1856, I became the first white man to cross southern Africa from the coast of Angola in the west to Quelimane on the coast of Mozambique in the east.

◆ ◆ ◆

When I returned to Britain in 1856, I found that I'd become a national hero. I was a famous explorer, and everybody wanted to meet me! So I was invited to give many talks about my travels. In addition, I wrote a book about my journey across Africa which became very popular. The LMS were very keen for me to return to Africa and continue preaching Christianity, but now my own purpose for being in Africa had changed. The slave trade was still going on there, and I hated it and wanted to stop it. So I asked the British Government to give me money for an <u>expedition</u> to explore the Zambezi River. I wanted to <u>navigate</u> the river and open it up for trading in <u>goods</u>. I hoped that this kind of trading would finally replace the terrible slave trade.

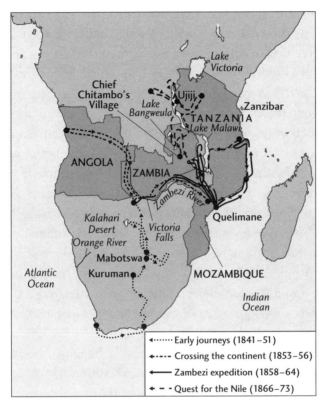

David Livingstone's Africa

The British Government agreed to give me money, and they <u>appointed</u> me as leader of the Zambezi Expedition. I had five British colleagues in my team, including my brother, as well as ten local Africans, and we sailed on a boat called the *Ma-Robert*. My plan was to explore the Zambezi from its <u>source</u> to the end, and prove that it was <u>navigable</u> all the way – in other words, that it was possible for boats to sail along it to the coast. But unfortunately the Zambezi Expedition was not a success. I was used to leading Africans, not people from my own country, and the British members of my team weren't used to my ways. Arguments started among the members of the team, and they said that the problems were often my fault.

In 1862, I suffered a terrible tragedy. My wife Mary joined our expedition, leaving our children in Britain. But three months later, she became ill with malaria, a disease carried by <u>mosquitoes</u>, and she died. It was terrible to lose the woman who had been my dear wife and friend. We buried Mary under a tree in the village of Chupanga, beside the Zambezi. We continued with our expedition, but it came to an end when we reached the Cahora Basso rapids, an area of the river where the water moved very fast over rocks. It was impossible to take a boat over these rapids, so we learned that the Zambezi was not navigable, as I'd hoped. However, we found land suitable for farming, as well as rivers and lakes where people could catch excellent fish.

◆ ◆ ◆

By now it was 1864, and I'd been away on the Zambezi Expedition for six years. The British Government were worried about how much the expedition was costing, and

I was ordered to return home. When I arrived in London, I gave a report about the expedition to the government, but they weren't very happy. The expedition had been very expensive, and I hadn't managed to find a navigable route along the Zambezi. Many newspapers wrote that the expedition had failed, and it was difficult for me to persuade the government to give me more money. But now I had an idea for a new expedition – to find the source of the River Nile. So in January 1866, I returned to Africa, this time to the island of Zanzibar.

In Zanzibar, I got a team of people together, including some men who'd been slaves in the past, and other men from different parts of Africa. However, problems started when some of my men began to leave me. Some even went back to Zanzibar and told the authorities there that I had died! In August 1866, I reached Lake Malawi, but by that time, most of my supplies had been stolen, including all my medicines. I was very weak and sick, and greatly in need of help. Ironically, I was rescued by the people I hated most – the slave traders. I sent a message to Zanzibar, asking for supplies to be sent to Ujiji, the oldest town in Western Tanzania. I travelled with the slave traders to Lake Mweru, arriving there in November 1867.

When I'd recovered, I continued exploring and travelled south. I found a river which at first I thought was the Nile, but actually it was another river, the Lualaba. In early 1869, while I was in the jungle, I became very ill again, and once more, slave traders helped me and saved my life. In March 1869, I finally reached Ujiji, but I found that all my supplies had been stolen. I became ill with cholera, a terrible disease, and my feet were very painful too. For the third time, I was helped by slave traders, who took me to a place called Bambara. I hadn't any supplies left, so I had to depend on local <u>tribes</u> to give me food. Finally I returned to Ujiji in October 1871.

♦ ◆ ♦

I hadn't been in contact with the world outside Africa for nearly six years, and for the last four years, my health had been very bad. As far as I knew, people in Britain believed that I was dead. I didn't think anyone was interested in finding me. But on 10th November 1871, a wonderful thing happened. My servant suddenly came running to tell me that a white man had arrived. To my great surprise, he knew who I was, and greeted me with a phrase that became very famous – 'Dr Livingstone, I <u>presume</u>?' This man's name was Henry Morton Stanley, and he was an American reporter who'd been sent to find me by the *New York Herald* newspaper. During the next six months, Stanley and I became good friends and we travelled to many places together.

Stanley tried hard to persuade me to leave Africa, but I always refused. I didn't want to leave until I'd achieved the purpose of my expedition – to find the source of the River Nile. So he left Africa, and went to Britain to tell the government that I was still alive. But I still had problems with my health, and on 1st May 1873, I died from an illness in Chief Chitambo's village, which is southeast of Lake Bangweulu in the country now known as Zambia. After my death, my two servants removed my heart and buried it under a tree near the place where I died. Then, amazingly, they carried my body for over a thousand miles to the coast, where it was returned to Britain.

My body was buried in Westminster Abbey in London as a national hero. However, not everything in my life had gone well, and I hadn't achieved all my hopes and dreams. I failed to open up the Zambezi River as a trade route and I hadn't found the source of the River Nile. Above all, I was very sorry that I hadn't been able to spend more time with my dear wife and children. But I'd <u>pioneered</u> ways into Africa and discovered new places, making it easier for people to come after me and develop education, <u>healthcare</u> and trade. Most important of all, I'd told people about the terrible slave trade in Africa, and I'd done everything I could to stop it.

The Life of David Livingstone

1813   David Livingstone was born in Blantyre, South Lanarkshire, Scotland.

1823   At the age of ten, he began working in Monteith's Blantyre cotton mill.

1836   David began studying medicine at Anderson's College and Glasgow University.

1838   He was accepted by the London Missionary Society. While completing his missionary training, he continued to study medicine.

1840–1841   He met Robert Moffat, a Scottish missionary. He travelled to Africa and worked as a missionary doctor at Kuruman.

1842–1844   David set up a missionary outpost at Mabotswa. After being attacked by a lion, he returned to Kuruman and met Mary Moffat, daughter of Robert.

1845   David and Mary married. They had six children over 13 years. Tragically, one daughter, Elizabeth, died when only two months old.

1849–1851   David and his family made two trips across the Kalahari Desert. On the second trip, David saw the upper part of the Zambezi River.

1852–1856   Mary and the children returned to Britain. David discovered a huge waterfall which he named Victoria Falls, and became the first European to cross southern Africa.

1856–1857   David returned to Britain as a national hero. He published *Missionary Travels and Researches in South Africa*. After this, he left the London Missionary Society because he wanted to do more exploring.

1858   He returned to Africa as head of the Zambezi Expedition.

1862   Mary joined the Zambezi Expedition, but shortly afterwards, she died of malaria and was buried next to the Zambezi.

1864–1865   After the expedition failed, David was ordered to return to Britain. He published *Narrative of an Expedition to the Zambezi and its Tributaries*.

1866–1871   He travelled to the island of Zanzibar, where he got together a team for an expedition to find the source of the River Nile. However, he became dangerously ill, although his life was saved several times by slave traders.

1871   Henry Morton Stanley, a reporter for the *New York Herald*, discovered David in the town of Ujiji, in western Tanzania.

1873   David died from an illness on 1st May 1873 in Chief Chitambo's Village, near Lake Bangweulu in the country now known as Zambia.

Yuri Gagarin

◆ ◆ ◆

1934–1968

the first man who went into space

I was a famous Soviet <u>cosmonaut</u> and <u>pioneer</u> of space travel. I was the first man to journey into space, and to complete an <u>orbit</u> of the Earth. I became an international hero. Some people called me 'the Columbus of space.'

◆ ◆ ◆

I was born on 9th March 1934 in Klushino, a small village 160 kilometres west of Moscow in the Soviet Union (the USSR) in the part now known as Russia. My village was near the town of Gzhatsk. I was the third of four children, and my parents worked on a collective farm, which was a group of farms managed by workers under the control of the government. When I was five years old, the Second World War began. During the war, German soldiers came and attacked our area, and forced my family to leave their home. In 1943, my older brother and sister were sent away from the Soviet Union, but I was only seven, so I was allowed to stay with my parents.

After the war, our family moved to Gzhatsk, where I received a basic education, paid for by the government. At school, I especially enjoyed mathematics and physics, and became very good at these subjects. In addition, one of my teachers, who had been a pilot in the war, <u>inspired</u> me to become interested in <u>astronomy</u>. I didn't know that this subject would be very useful in my future career! After I left school, I became an <u>apprentice</u> in a factory, working with metal. As part of my training, I attended the technical college in the city of Saratov, on the River Volga. I was very keen to become a pilot, so I joined a flying club, and learned to fly light planes.

As soon as possible, I joined the Soviet <u>Air Force</u> and started training at the Orenburg School for Pilots. I learned to fly a MiG-15, a Soviet fighter-plane, and I also did some <u>parachute</u> training. While at Orenburg, I met a lovely girl called Valentina Ivanovna Goryacheva (Valya) at a dance at the school. I fell in love with Valya, who was training to be a nurse, and we married in November 1957. On the same day, I graduated from the Pilot School with very high honours. Later, Valya and I had two daughters. Although my work was always very important to me, I very much enjoyed family life and being a father, and my dear wife and family were never far from my thoughts.

◆ ◆ ◆

After graduating, I was sent on several <u>missions</u>. First, I was ordered to go to Loustari Airbase in the Murmansk Oblast, an area in the far north-west of the Soviet Union, close to the border with Norway. There I became an expert fighter-pilot, and learned to fly planes very fast in difficult and dangerous weather conditions. There is very little space inside a fighter-plane, but I was only 1.57 metres tall, so I was quite comfortable inside one. I completed all my missions successfully, and in 1959 I was <u>promoted</u> to Second Lieutenant. However, although I enjoyed flying, my real interest was always in space travel. I'd followed the <u>progress</u> of the Soviet Union's space programme, and I was sure that they were planning to send a man into space soon.

My great <u>ambition</u> was to be that man, so I applied to join the Cosmonaut Training Programme. This trained people to command, pilot or serve as a crew member on a <u>spacecraft</u>. The programme was top secret, because of the 'Space Race', the strong competition between the USSR and the USA. Each country was very keen to be the world leader in space travel, and be first to put a man on the Moon. The President of the USA, John F. Kennedy, thought it was important for the US to win the 'Space Race', but the Russian leader, Nikita Khrushchev, wanted the USSR to be first. He didn't want the Americans to find out what progress the USSR was making, so the Soviet cosmonauts were trained in secret.

In 1960, I was told that I was one of 20 men selected for cosmonaut training. Valya and I moved to Star City, the area of Moscow Oblast where the cosmonauts are trained. All the men knew that only one of us would be selected for the first <u>voyage</u> into space. We had to go through all sorts of tests, to find out if we were fit. Physical fitness is very important for a cosmonaut. Your body has to be very strong to cope with the force that presses on you when a spacecraft is <u>launched</u>, the great heat inside the spacecraft and then the feeling of weighing nothing. Mental fitness is important too, as you have to be smart and able to think fast. You also have to stay cool and keep calm when things go wrong.

◆ ◆ ◆

Our training was long and difficult, with many weeks of test flights and experiments. However, I was delighted when I learned that I was the man chosen for the dangerous voyage into space. The trainers liked me because in addition to my skills, I was always cheerful, and I had a good sense of humour. The chief designer of the programme was a brilliant engineer called Sergei Korolev. Korolev had planned and directed the <u>launch</u> of *Sputnik 1*, the world's first <u>artificial satellite</u>, in October 1957. This satellite, which was the size of a large ball, had been sent into space and had circled the Earth for 98 minutes. People all over the world had admired this wonderful achievement by the Soviet space programme.

Sputnik 1 had been followed a month later in November 1957 by *Sputnik 2*. This carried a dog called Laika, the first living creature to be sent into space. Unfortunately, poor Laika didn't survive more than a few hours in space because of the great heat in the spacecraft. But Korolev didn't give up, and now he had an even more <u>ambitious</u> plan – to send a human being into space for the first time. He and his team had designed a spacecraft called *Vostok 1*. After I became the first person in space, I became the 'face' of the *Vostok 1* project. People saw my picture in the newspapers and they knew my name. But Sergei Korolev and his team were the clever men behind the project, the people who had engineered and designed it.

The day chosen for the launch of *Vostok 1* was 12th April 1961. The launch was due to take place at Baikonur Cosmodrome in Kazakhstan, the same place where *Sputnik 1* had been launched. This area was built by the Soviet Union in the late 1950s, and is the world's first and largest place for launching spacecraft. Just before I climbed up into *Vostok 1* for the launch, I gave a speech. I said that I felt great happiness because I was going to do what other people had only dreamed about. I was going to be the first person in history to make a voyage into space, and go where no man had gone before. I was proud and happy, but I also knew that I'd been given a great responsibility by my country.

◆ ◆ ◆

I was <u>strapped</u> into the capsule, the part at the top of the main spacecraft, with many thoughts going through my mind. Nobody really knew what the effects of space on the human body would be, and many things could go wrong. I was the first human being to go into space, and I really didn't know whether I would live or die. Perhaps I would even become <u>stranded</u> in space! I thought about my dear wife and family, waiting for me at home, but I was more excited than afraid. As *Vostok 1* took off from the Earth with a great noise and I was launched into space, Korolev and his team in the control room heard me shout, 'Let's go!'

I completed a single orbit around the Earth, flying at a height of over 300 kilometres and reaching a speed of almost 28,000 kilometres per hour. It was truly amazing to see our beautiful planet Earth from space. When *Vostok 1* entered Earth's atmosphere again, I felt as if I was in a cloud of fire,

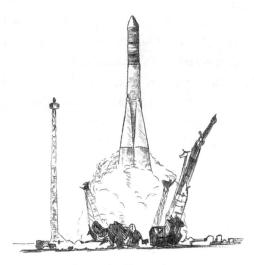

Vostok 1 took off on 12th April 1961

rushing down. Korolev had planned that my spacecraft and I should land in different places. So, seven kilometres above Earth, I ejected from *Vostok 1* – I freed myself and was pushed out of the spacecraft with great force. *Vostok 1* landed at 10.55 a.m. after <u>orbiting</u> the Earth for 108 minutes. Meanwhile, I <u>parachuted</u> down and landed at the village of Uzmoriye, near the Volga River, not far from Saratov.

Unfortunately, my parachute had brought me down to Earth almost 300 kilometres from the planned landing place. So I needed to let my team in Moscow know that I'd landed safely. Then something very funny happened; I saw a woman and a little girl coming towards me, and I waved my arms and shouted to attract their attention. However, they were amazed by the sight of this strange creature who had fallen from the sky wearing an orange spacesuit and a big white <u>space helmet</u>. They were convinced that I must be mad, or perhaps a foreign spy. It wasn't easy to persuade them that I was a Russian too, and that I needed to find the nearest phone. I told them I had to call Moscow with the news that I'd returned from space!

After my return to Earth, I became very famous. I had to walk in Red Square, the main square in Moscow, in front of hundreds of thousands of people. This made me more nervous than my space voyage! I became a hero in my country, and I received many medals and titles, including Hero of the Soviet Union, the highest honour. My trip into space was not only a success for Soviet engineering and design, but also for the politicians in the Communist Party, who had supported the Cosmonaut Training Programme. The news spread around the world like fire. 'Man in space!' said the *London Evening News*, and other newspapers called me the 'Columbus of space'.

Valya and I made international tours to 28 countries, and I was welcomed everywhere as a modern-day hero. I became an 'ambassador of goodwill' for the USSR, talking about the achievements of the Soviet Union. I received political honours

too. In 1962, I was chosen as a member of the Supreme Soviet of the Soviet Union, the Soviet parliament. I became a Lieutenant Colonel of the Soviet Air Force on 12th June 1962, and I was promoted to Colonel on 6th November 1963. I also returned to Star City, where I became assistant training director of the Star City Cosmonaut Training Centre.

Over the next seven years, I worked on spacecraft design, and trained other cosmonauts including Valentina Tereshkova, who on 16th June 1963 became the first woman in space. Although I wanted to make another journey into space myself, unfortunately this never happened, so I trained as a fighter-pilot again. On 7th March 1968, I was flying a MiG-15 on a training flight from Chkalovsky Air Base. The weather was bad, and our plane crashed, killing me and my instructor. I was only 34, and many people thought that my death was a national tragedy.

Although I only went into space once in my life, I showed the way for others to follow. As a result of my space voyage on 12th April 1961, President John F. Kennedy made a speech to Congress in the US government on 25th May. He asked Congress for 22 billion dollars to develop the Apollo Space Programme, the American Space Programme, and they agreed to give him the money. On 20th July 1969, the Americans Neil Armstrong and Edwin Eugene 'Buzz' Aldrin became the first men to walk on the Moon, and the USA won the 'Space Race.' Tragically, I didn't live to see that day myself, but an area on the Moon was named Gagarin to honour me, the first man who went into space. The town of Gzhatsk, near the village where I was born, was also given the name Gagarin in my honour.

The Life of Yuri Alekseyevich Gagarin

1934   Yuri Alekseyevich Gagarin was born in the village of Klushino in the Soviet Union (the USSR), in the part now known as Russia.

1946   Yuri's family moved to Gzhatsk following the end of the Second World War. After finishing school, Yuri became an apprentice in a factory, working with metal. He also attended the technical college in Saratov, where he joined a flying club and flew light planes.

1955   He joined the Soviet Air Force and entered the Orenburg School for Pilots. He learned to fly a MiG-15 fighter-plane, and met Valentina Ivanovna Goryachova (Valya).

1957   Yuri married Valya and they later had two daughters.

1958–1959   Yuri was sent to Loustari Airbase in the north-west of the Soviet Union. He was promoted to Second Lieutenant in the Soviet Air Force.

1960   He applied to join the Cosmonaut Training Programme, and was chosen out of 20 men to be the first man to journey into space. He and Valya moved to Star City. Yuri met Sergei Korolev, the brilliant engineer and designer of the *Vostok 1* spacecraft.

1961   On 12th April, Yuri became the first human to journey into space in *Vostok 1* and orbit the Earth. After the flight, he toured the world as an international hero, speaking about the successful achievements of the Soviet Union.

1962–1968   He served as a member of the Supreme Soviet of the Soviet Union. He became Lieutenant Colonel of the Soviet Air Force and was later promoted to Colonel. He became assistant training director of the Star City Cosmonaut Training Base and also trained again as a fighter-pilot.

1968   While on a training flight in a MiG-15 on 7th March, Yuri's plane crashed. He died aged 34, in Novosyolovo, in the Soviet Union.

◆ Glossary ◆

adventure UNCOUNTABLE NOUN
Adventure is getting involved in events that are unusual, exciting, and perhaps dangerous.

air force COUNTABLE NOUN
An **air force** is the part of a country's military organization that is concerned with fighting in the air.

ambassador COUNTABLE NOUN
An **ambassador** is an important official living in a foreign country who represents the government of his or her own country.

ambition COUNTABLE NOUN
If you have an **ambition** to achieve something, you want very much to achieve it.

ambitious ADJECTIVE
An **ambitious** idea or plan is on a large scale and needs a lot of work to be successful.

appoint TRANSITIVE VERB
If you **appoint** someone **to** a job or post, you formally choose them for it.

apprentice COUNTABLE NOUN
An **apprentice** is a person who works with someone in order to learn their skill.
to become apprenticed to someone If a young person becomes apprenticed to someone, they go to work for them in order to learn their skill.

artificial satellite COUNTABLE NOUN
An **artificial satellite** is a man-made object that is sent into space, for example to forecast the weather or to send television or telephone signals.

ashore ADVERB
Something that comes **ashore** comes from the sea onto the shore.

astronomical ADJECTIVE
Astronomical instruments and equipment are used for studying the stars, planets, and other natural objects in space.

astronomy UNCOUNTABLE NOUN
Astronomy is the scientific study of the stars, planets, and other natural objects in space.

authority UNCOUNTABLE NOUN
Authority is the right to command and control other people.
PLURAL NOUN
The **authorities** are official organizations, especially government ones, that have the power to make decisions.

camel COUNTABLE NOUN
A **camel** is a desert animal with one or two humps on its back.

Catholic Church SINGULAR NOUN
The Catholic Church is the branch of the Christian Church that accepts the Pope as its leader.

claim TRANSITIVE VERB
If you **claim** something such as money, property, or land, you ask for it because you have a right to it.

cosmonaut COUNTABLE NOUN
A **cosmonaut** is an astronaut from the former Soviet Union.

court COUNTABLE NOUN
The **court** of a king or queen is the place where he or she lives and works.

disaster COUNTABLE NOUN
A **disaster** is a very bad accident such as an earthquake or a plane crash.

empire COUNTABLE NOUN
An **empire** is a group of countries controlled by one powerful country.

establish TRANSITIVE VERB
If someone **establishes** an organization or a system, they create it.

expedition COUNTABLE NOUN
An **expedition** is a journey made for a particular purpose such as exploration.

fleet COUNTABLE NOUN
A **fleet** is an organized group of ships.

goods PLURAL NOUN
Goods are things that are made to be sold.

goodwill UNCOUNTABLE NOUN
Goodwill is a friendly or helpful attitude towards other people, countries, or organizations.

healthcare UNCOUNTABLE NOUN
Healthcare refers to systems and services for keeping people healthy and looking after them when they are ill.

hippopotamus COUNTABLE NOUN
A **hippopotamus** is a very large African animal with short legs and thick, hairless skin. Hippopotamuses live in and near rivers.

HMS COUNTABLE NOUN
HMS is used before the names of ships in the British Royal Navy. **HMS** is an abbreviation for 'Her Majesty's Ship' or 'His Majesty's Ship'.

holy ADJECTIVE
Something that is **holy** is considered to be special because it relates to God or to a particular religion.

impressed ADJECTIVE
If you are **impressed**, you feel great admiration for something.

inspire TRANSITIVE VERB
If someone or something **inspires** you to do something, they give you the idea or motivation to do it.

ironically ADVERB
You use **ironically** to draw attention to a situation which is odd or amusing because it involves a contrast.

judgment COUNTABLE NOUN
A **judgment** is an opinion that you have or express after thinking carefully about something.

launch TRANSITIVE VERB
To **launch** a rocket, missile, or satellite means to send it into the air or into space.
VARIABLE NOUN
The **launch** of a rocket, missile, or satellite is when it is sent into the air or into space.

magnificent ADJECTIVE
Something or someone that is **magnificent** is extremely good, beautiful, or impressive.

merchant COUNTABLE NOUN
A **merchant** is a person whose business is buying or selling goods in large quantities.

mill COUNTABLE NOUN
A **mill** is a factory used for making and processing materials such as steel, wool, or cotton.

mission COUNTABLE NOUN
A **mission** is a special journey made by a military aeroplane or space rocket.

missionary COUNTABLE NOUN
A **missionary** is a Christian who has been sent to a foreign country to teach people about Christianity.

mosque COUNTABLE NOUN
A **mosque** is a building where Muslims go to worship.

mosquito COUNTABLE NOUN
Mosquitoes are small flying insects which bite people in order to suck their blood.

native ADJECTIVE
A person who is **native** to a country or region is a person who was born there.

navigable ADJECTIVE
A **navigable** river is wide and deep enough for a boat to travel along safely.

navigate TRANSITIVE VERB
When someone **navigates** a ship or an aircraft somewhere, they decide which course it should follow and steer it there.

navigator COUNTABLE NOUN
The **navigator** on an aircraft or ship is the person whose job is to work out the direction in which the aircraft or ship should be travelling.

navy COUNTABLE NOUN
A country's **navy** is the part of its armed forces that fights at sea.

New World PROPER NOUN
The New World is used to refer to the continents of North and South America.

official ADJECTIVE
If you describe someone's reason for something as the **official** reason, you are suggesting that it is probably not true, but is used because the real one is a secret.
COUNTABLE NOUN
An **official** is a person who holds a position of authority in an organization.

officially ADVERB
If someone does something **officially**, what they do is approved by the government or by someone in authority.

orbit VARIABLE NOUN
An **orbit** is the curved path followed by an object going round a planet, a moon, or the Sun.
TRANSITIVE VERB
If something **orbits** a planet, a moon, or the Sun, it goes round and round it.

outpost COUNTABLE NOUN
An **outpost** is a small settlement in a foreign country or in a distant area.

ox (oxen) COUNTABLE NOUN
An **ox** is a castrated bull.

parachute COUNTABLE NOUN
A **parachute** is a device that enables a person to jump from an aircraft and float safely to the ground. It consists of a large piece of thin cloth attached to your body by strings.
INTRANSITIVE VERB
If someone **parachutes**, they jump from an aircraft using a parachute.

pilgrim COUNTABLE NOUN
A **pilgrim** is a person who makes a journey to a holy place.

pilgrimage VARIABLE NOUN
If someone makes a **pilgrimage** to a place, they make a journey there because the place is holy according to their religion.

pioneer COUNTABLE NOUN
A **pioneer** in a new activity is one of the first people to do it.
TRANSITIVE VERB
Someone who **pioneers** a new activity or way of doing something is one of the first people to do it.

pirate COUNTABLE NOUN
Pirates are sailors who attack other ships and steal property from them.

porcelain UNCOUNTABLE NOUN
Porcelain is a hard, shiny substance made by heating clay. It is used to make cups, plates, and ornaments.

preach TRANSITIVE VERB
If someone **preaches** a belief, he or she tries to persuade other people to accept it by telling them about it.

preacher COUNTABLE NOUN
A **preacher** is a person who gives talks about religion, especially as part of a church service.

presume TRANSITIVE VERB
If you **presume** that something is the case, you think that it is true, although you are not certain.

priest COUNTABLE NOUN
A **priest** is a person who has religious duties in a place where people worship.

progress SINGULAR NOUN
The **progress** of a situation or action is the way in which it develops.

promote TRANSITIVE VERB
If someone **is promoted**, they are given a more important job in the organization they work for.

run into (runs into, running into, ran into, run into) PHRASAL VERB
If you **run into** problems or difficulties, you unexpectedly begin to experience them.

sail
to set sail When a ship **sets sail**, it leaves a port.

scholar COUNTABLE NOUN
A **scholar** is a person who studies an academic subject and knows a lot about it.

shore COUNTABLE NOUN
The **shore** of a sea, lake, or wide river is the land along the edge of it.

silk VARIABLE NOUN
Silk is a very smooth, fine cloth made from a substance produced by a kind of moth.

Silk Road PROPER NOUN
The **Silk Road** was a route through Asia used by traders, soldiers, and other people in the past.

skilful ADJECTIVE
Someone who is **skilful** at something does it very well.

slave COUNTABLE NOUN
A **slave** is a person who is owned by another person and has to work for that person without pay.

source SINGULAR NOUN
The **source** of a river or stream is the place where it begins.

spacecraft COUNTABLE NOUN
A **spacecraft** is a rocket or other vehicle that can travel in space.

space helmet COUNTABLE NOUN
A **space helmet** is something that astronauts wear on their heads when they are travelling in space.

spice VARIABLE NOUN
A **spice** is a part of a plant, or a powder made from that part, which you put in food to give it flavour.

stranded ADJECTIVE
If you are **stranded**, you cannot leave a place, for example because of bad weather.

strap TRANSITIVE VERB
If you **strap** someone somewhere, you fasten them there with a narrow piece of leather, cloth, or other material.

survey TRANSITIVE VERB
To **survey** a building or area of land means to examine it and measure it, usually in order to make a map of it.

surveyor COUNTABLE NOUN
A **surveyor** is a person whose job is to survey land.

trade UNCOUNTABLE NOUN
Trade is the activity of buying, selling, or exchanging goods or services.
INTRANSITIVE VERB
When people or countries **trade**, they buy, sell, or exchange goods or services.

trader COUNTABLE NOUN
A **trader** is a person whose job is to buy and sell a particular type of goods.

tribe COUNTABLE NOUN
A **tribe** is a group of people of the same race, language, and customs, especially in a developing country.

voyage COUNTABLE NOUN
A **voyage** is a long journey on a ship or in a spacecraft.

Collins
English Readers

THE AMAZING PEOPLE READERS SERIES:

Level 1

Amazing Inventors
978-0-00-754494-3

Amazing Leaders
978-0-00-754492-9

Amazing Entrepreneurs and Business People *(May 2014)*
978-0-00-754501-8

Amazing Women *(May 2014)*
978-0-00-754493-6

Amazing Performers *(June 2014)*
978-0-00-754508-7

Level 2

Amazing Aviators
978-0-00-754495-0

Amazing Architects and Artists
978-0-00-754496-7

Amazing Composers *(May 2014)*
978-0-00-754502-5

Amazing Mathematicians *(May 2014)*
978-0-00-754503-2

Amazing Medical People *(June 2014)*
978-0-00-754509-4

Level 3

Amazing Explorers
978-0-00-754497-4

Amazing Writers
978-0-00-754498-1

Amazing Philanthropists *(May 2014)*
978-0-00-754504-9

Amazing Performers *(May 2014)*
978-0-00-754505-6

Amazing Scientists *(June 2014)*
978-0-00-754510-0

Level 4

Amazing Thinkers and Humanitarians
978-0-00-754499-8

Amazing Scientists
978-0-00-754500-1

Amazing Writers *(May 2014)*
978-0-00-754506-3

Amazing Leaders *(May 2014)*
978-0-00-754507-0

Amazing Entrepreneurs and Business People *(June 2014)*
978-0-00-754511-7

Visit **www.collinselt.com/readers** for language activities, teacher's notes, and to find out more about the series.